To Christian and all the animals that enrich our lives
—A. B. and J. R.

Henry Holt and Company, LLC
Publishers since 1866
175 Fifth Avenue
New York, New York 10010
www.HenryHoltKids.com

Library of Congress Control Number: 2009927584
ISBN 978-0-8050-9182-3
First American Edition—2009
Printed in May 2009 in the United States of America by Worzalla,
Stevens Point, Wisconsin, on acid-free paper. ∞

1 3 5 7 9 10 8 6 4 2

Photo credits: Christian's parents © John Rendall; London photos © Derek Cattani; Leith Hill and Africa photos © Derek Cattani / Born Free Foundation; reunion photo © Tony Fitzjohn / George Adamson Wildlife Preservation Trust.

CHRISTIAN THE LION

Based on the true story
of Anthony (Ace) Bourke,
John Rendall, and
Christian the Lion

Henry Holt and Company
NEW YORK

This is the story of our friend Christian the lion. We met him a long time ago, when the world was a very different place. We first saw Christian in a department store. He was living in a cage. We didn't think it was right to leave him there and we thought we could give him a better home, so he came to live with us. This is his scrapbook. This is his story.

from John and Ace

My Family

This is my dad.

This is my mom.

And this is me!

We have been to
**ILFRACOMBE
ZOO PARK**
top of
Marlborough Road

Finding a Home

I have lived in some very exciting places with some really interesting people.

My first home was in Ilfracombe Zoo Park. It is very near the sea.

SCOTLAND

NORTHERN IRELAND

IRELAND

WALES   ENGLAND

Ilfracombe

London

After the zoo, I lived in this grand building. It's a big store in London, called Harrods. And that's where I met my two best friends.

My Best Friends

John and Ace quickly became my friends. They visited me a lot when I lived at Harrods and spent a long time playing with me. When they asked if I'd like to live with them, I said, "Yes, please!" right away.

This is John.   And this is Ace!

John and Ace lived above a store. They said people came to look at me just as much as they came to look at the furniture for sale!

From this spot on the stairs I could watch everything that went on!

Underneath my paw is my favorite toy pig.

It wasn't long before I knew I was going to be very happy living here.

Exploring!

The store was like having a furniture jungle to prowl around, and the apartment upstairs was full of exciting things to play with.

Tables were great to lie on!

Televisions were tempting to climb on.

Trash baskets were such fun!

You can always find something interesting in a drawer!

Sometimes I just watched the world go by.

This is me . . . on the prowl.

I was never happy about bathtime, though.

New Friends and Games

I made lots of new friends!

Hmm, who do you think is the fluffiest?

I used to go to a garden every afternoon. There was always someone new to meet and plenty of great games to play ...

1 ... 2 ... 3 ... I tried to count them but they just wouldn't stay still!

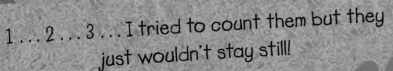

You're very tall. I hope I grow as big
as you one day!

Soccer was so much fun!
Sometimes I even let John and Ace win.

Out and About

I went to some really fun places. John and Ace said that I'd become famous!

This is me when I went on the radio. It was very early in the morning and I was so sleepy, I'm not sure I gave my best performance.

On special occasions we went out for dinner at the best restaurants.

This is a famous statue in London. He must have been a very important lion. I wonder if we're related?

This was the day the king of the road met the king of the jungle! James Hunt was a very fast racing driver.

As much as I loved going on trips, I was always happy when it was time to go home at the end of the day.

Getting Too Big

Then things started to feel different. Everything seemed like it was getting smaller. But maybe it was me getting bigger?

I could only hide under the biggest pieces of furniture.

I began to realize that I was getting too big to stay with John and Ace. They knew it, too. We'd called some safari parks to see if maybe I could live with them, but then . . .

I met two special new friends.

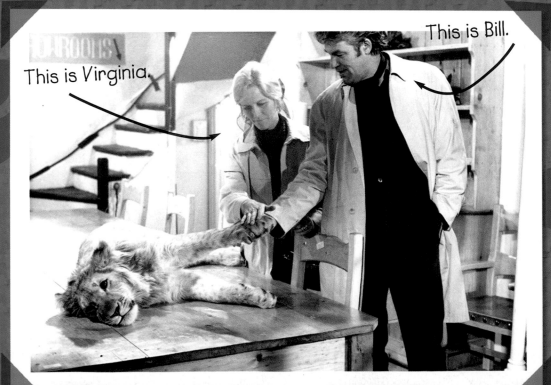

This is Virginia.

This is Bill.

Bill and Virginia had come into the store to buy a desk, but instead they found me! They knew all about lions and taught me that lions didn't usually live in stores, or have best friends who were human. Lions usually lived in the wild in a country called Africa. It sounded like an amazing place.

They told me about a very special lioness named Elsa. She had also lived with humans. Two of Bill and Virginia's friends had taught her how to live in the wild. Maybe they could help me to learn the same thing.

John and Ace were very happy! Teaching me to be wild and live with other lions was what they had always hoped for.

I'm sure my bottom used to fit on this step!

ELSA THE LIONESS

Bill and Virginia Travers were actors who had starred in a film called *Born Free*. It was the true story of a girl lion called Elsa. When she was little, her mom died. She went to live with two humans, George and Joy Adamson, in Africa. Very slowly they taught Elsa how to survive outside, in the open spaces of Africa. When she was ready to leave their home, they set her free. She had a very happy life in the wild. Bill promised John and Ace that he would tell George all about me. Then maybe I could learn to live free, just like Elsa!

A Home in the Country

Bill and Virginia lived in a very big house in the countryside. There was grass and trees and space for me to run around. It was amazing! I soon realized I wasn't a city cat anymore.

From living inside the store, this was one step closer to my new life in Africa. I got used to living outside. I started to grow much bigger and my hair got longer. I even tried a roar.

ROAR, ROAR!

SCOTLAND

NORTHERN IRELAND

IRELAND

WALES

ENGLAND

This is London. This is Leith Hill in Surrey where Bill and Virginia lived.

Look at my mane!

If this is what it was going to be like in Africa, then I knew I was going to be a very happy lion.

John and Ace came to stay here with me. This is my caravan where I used to sleep.

Learning New Tricks

One day I discovered a great new game!

I'm sure Ace won't mind if I borrow this blanket for a bit.

This is great fun!

Who turned out the lights?

Oh! There you all are!

Where am I going?

How did I end up in this bush?

Going on a Journey

I had grown used to my life in the countryside. But the more I learned about Africa, the more excited I was to be going there.

This is George Adamson.

The flight would take 15 hours. I would travel inside a large box. It was big enough for me to sit up and to turn around in. John and Ace helped me get used to spending time inside it so I wouldn't be scared when it was time to leave.

PASSPORT

What I've learned about being a lion:

- Lions are the BIGGEST cats in Africa.
- Wild lions like to live in Africa, where there is lots of space.
- They like to catch and eat animals such as antelope, zebra, and buffalo.
- Lions live in large families, called prides.
- Because it is so hot where they live, lions usually sleep in the day and hunt at night, when it is cooler.
- Rubbing heads is a lion's way of saying "Hello!"

That's me inside my box!

This is England, where I used to live.

This is Kenya, my new home.

George wanted to make a family of lions. For a little while we would all live together in a camp. Then we would move into the wild, but George would stay close by until he was sure we were ready to live by ourselves.

Life in Camp

My new home! Africa was very different. It was very hot and dry. I had never seen so much open space. This is our camp; it was where I would learn how to be wild.

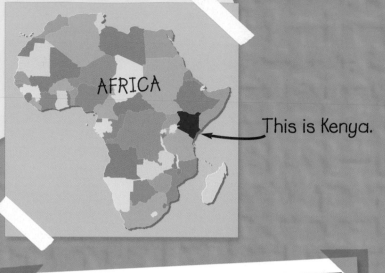

AFRICA

This is Kenya.

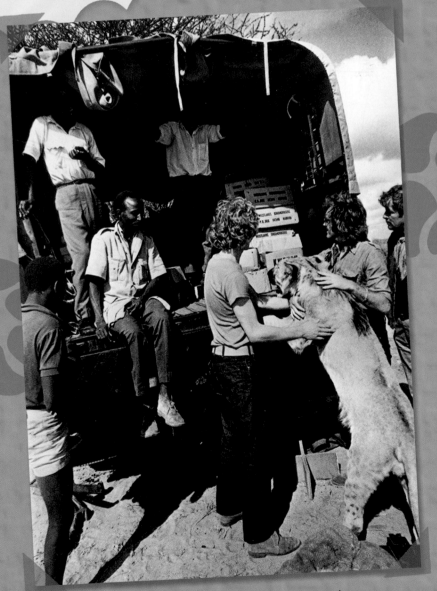

The first night in camp I slept with John and Ace. I wanted to make sure they weren't scared of being in a new place.

So many people came to meet us when we arrived!

I felt at home right away.

Me, taking a catnap.

Look at that space! I couldn't wait to explore.

The only way to keep cool was in the shade!

Should this be holding the tent up?

Making New Friends

After I'd been living here for about a week, George brought two new lions to the camp. He hoped that we would form a pride and become a family.

This little cub is Katania. We made friends instantly.

She could be a bit mischievous though! Look, she's trying to steal my dinner!

This is Boy. He was a very tough lion. He was much bigger than me, and I have to say I was a bit scared of him the first time we met. There was a lot of growling and roaring. It was a long time before we became friends.

Learning to Live in the Wild

We started to spend more and more time outside the camp so that one day I would be ready to move into the wild.

John, Ace, and George took me on long walks outside the camp so I could get used to Africa.

On one of our first walks I spotted a *gombi* (which looks like a cow).

This is me starting to stalk it like a real wild lion! George said he didn't think I would have any trouble learning to be wild.

More Adventures

There were some sassy baboons
on the other side of the river!

John and Ace often went for a swim.
I preferred to watch them from the shade.

Is that another lion in there? No!
It's just my reflection!

Another catnap. Learning to be wild
can be tough work, you know!

Very
soon, my
paws grew tough,
I got used to the heat, and
I was spending more time outside the
camp with Boy and Katania. We all knew it
was nearly time for John and Ace
to go back to their home.
They knew they had
helped me find mine.

Time to Say Good-bye

Saying good-bye to John and Ace was hard, but they knew how happy I was to be in Africa. I think they were pleased that they could finally give me the life they'd always wanted to.

John and Ace knew that George and Boy could look after me, and that soon I would be able to look after myself.

Here we are, three friends walking off into the sunset.

A year after saying good-bye, we came back to Kenya to visit Christian. Although it had been a long time, George thought he would still remember us. It was very hot. George called his name. Suddenly he appeared, standing proudly on top of a large rock. He stared at us for a while. After what felt like ages, we both called his name and waited. And then, Christian came bounding toward us. He <u>did</u> remember us! We felt so happy and so proud. Christian was still our wonderful friend.

from

John and Ace